The Usborne Book of

NIGHT TIME

Laura Cowan

Illustrated by Bonnie Pang

Designed by Amy Manning

USBORNE QUICKLINKS

For links to websites where you can watch fireflies flash, see auroras
dance in the sky and discover lots more about night time, go to
www.usborne.com/quicklinks and type in the title of this book.
Please follow the internet safety guidelines at the Usborne Quicklinks
website. We recommend that children are supervised while on the internet.

CONTENTS

4-5   GOODNIGHT?

6-7   LIGHTS-OUT FACTORY

8-9   BEYOND THE TOWN...

10-11   BEEP BEEP! TOOT TOOT!

12-13   PARP, PARRRRRRRRRRP!

14-15   NIGHT BENEATH THE WAVES

16-17   FOREST OF THE NIGHT

18-19   NIGHT LIGHTS

20-21   FAR NORTH

22-23   STARLIGHT, STAR BRIGHT

24-25   OUTBACK

26-27   CITIES NEVER SLEEP

28-29   IS THERE NIGHT IN SPACE?

30-31   GOOD MORNING!

32   INDEX

Turn the page to explore the world at NIGHT...

The Moon looks different on different nights. Sometimes it's big and round, and sometimes it's just a little sliver.

G'night, mate!

GOODNIGHT?

It's getting DARK. But night isn't ONLY for sleeping – lots of other things are happening, too...

Goodnight, Sun!

Birds are getting ready for bed.

Who's this awake?

MEOW   Cats are just starting to be BUSY.

The police have things to do. They're driving around on patrol.

Twit-twoo!

Foxes and owls wake up for a night of hunting and scavenging.

Mice are awake, too, but they need to WATCH OUT.

It's bedtime for children.

I want to finish this chapter!

I'm staying up late to talk to my friend. She lives on the other side of the world.

Sizzle

Izzzz

This doctor is working NIGHT SHIFTS at the hospital.

I sleep in the daytime.

One last walk before bed!

WOOF WOOF

5

LIGHTS-OUT FACTORY

Some factories are JUST as busy at night as during the day. They have SUPER strong workers who can work with the LIGHTS OUT. They're ROBOT workers.

Big powerful robots build cars. I'm checking everything's running smoothly, but I need to stay out of their way so they can do their work without hurting me by mistake.

I'm recharging my battery. Zzzzzz!

We don't need lights to see. We're robots!

Bip bop

Beep meep

Bzzzzzzz

Fzzzzzzzzzzzz

I'll be back at work soon.

I'm here to fix the robots if they break.

VRRRRRRRRRRRRRRM

I'm a delivery robot. Beep beep!

BEEP BEEP! TOOT TOOT!

Lots of vehicles keep moving through the night to get people, goods and even pizzas where they need to go.

It's easier for big trucks to get around when the roads are emptier.

BEEP BEEP!

A sleeper train full of sleeping passengers whizzes out of the city...

...past mountains and fields, on its way to new places.

Zzz

Zzzzzzzzz

ZZOOOOOOOOOMMMM

I'm going to see my grandchildren. They live far away.

This container train carries all sorts of goods across the country to the port.

PARRRRRRRRRRRP

When it arrives, the containers are taken off the train and loaded onto a huge ship.

What's in this container ship?

It's carrying lots of new cars. The biggest ships can carry 18,000 cars at once!

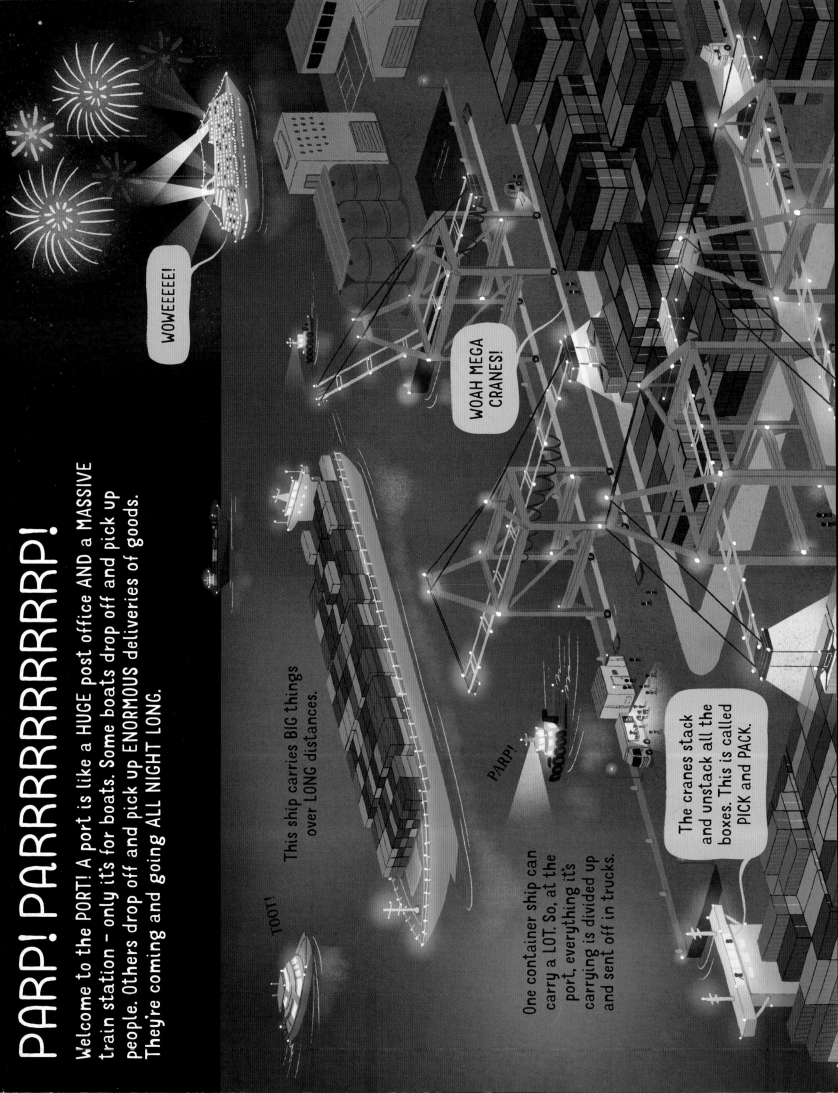

NIGHT BENEATH THE WAVES

In shallow waters in warm seas, strange creatures called CORALS come alive at night. And for each type of coral there is one night, once a year - when the temperature's right and the Moon is big - when they make NEW CORALS.

On that night, the corals release eggs into the water.

They're carried along by the waves until they fall to the bottom of the sea and stick to a rock FOREVER.

These rocky shapes that look like plants are all different types of CORALS.

POP

Lots and LOTS of corals together make a REEF.

The eggs become NEW corals. They grow their skeletons around themselves, on the OUTSIDE of their bodies.

POP

MINI fish

On the inside of a coral is its fleshy, squishy, moving body - called a POLYP.

Coral polyps wake up at night and wriggle their tentacles out to feed. And, tonight, to release eggs.

FOREST OF THE NIGHT

Now we're in a dense forest, FULL of creatures.
Can you see their eyes WATCHING you?

Uh oh... CLOUDED LEOPARDS prowl at night.

We can LEAP, too – watch out below!

Clouded leopards can climb STRAIGHT DOWN.

I'm sneaking up on birds, snakes and squirrels to POUNCE on and EAT – mmm mmm MMM.

Wheeeeeee!

Tarsiers are TINY, but they can jump a long way.

Chirrup!

YUCK! PONGY! That MASSIVE flower STINKS. None of the animals down here will eat it!

Greater mouse deer, oh hello!

The Rafflesia flower smells HORRIBLE and it only blooms at night.

This sun bear is asleep now. But it might wake up and look for food.

Ooh look, here's a Hose's civet. They are VERY RARE and not many people have seen one.

GRUNT
GRUNT

Bearded pig

SNUFFLE
SNUFFLE

Pangolin and BABY pangolin

NIGHT LIGHTS

Night isn't always dark. Not when some creatures light up the night THEMSELVES.

IN THE UNDERGROWTH are...

...GLOW-IN-THE-DARK mushrooms...

FLASH

...and insects, too.

FLASH

IN THE SEA are bright blue sparkles of light – tiny sea creatures called PHYTOPLANKTON.

Woah! Dude!

The phytoplankton make blue light when they are upset by too many waves... or surfers.

IN THE WOODS are hundreds
of tiny flecks of LIGHT.
They're FIREFLIES.

FLASH

FLASH

Fireflies are really BEETLES
that FLASH to say to other
fireflies, HELLO, I'm looking
for a FRIEND.

Their bottoms
are lit up!

But when BABY fireflies
flash, it's a message to other
creatures, DON'T EAT ME!
I'M POISONOUS!

FLASH

FLASH

IN SOUTHEAST ASIA lives a type of snail –
Quantula striata – the only land snail in the
WHOLE WORLD that can flash.

Our eggs flash!

FLASH

Like fireflies, their
flashes are probably a
way of talking, a way
of saying, HIYA or I'M
NOT A SNACK!

And baby snails
like me flash, too!

When the snails grow up,
some can't flash any more.

In the height of summer, for about two months, the Sun NEVER goes down – not even at MIDNIGHT.

Midnight Sun

Reindeer's eyes turn gold in summer when the Sun returns.

Most owls hunt in the dark, but in summer, snowy owls have no choice. They HAVE to hunt in sunlight.

Argh, I don't like sunshine. The hares down there can see me hunting them.

When the snow has melted, Arctic foxes and hares grow brown fur to blend in better with the undergrowth.

You can run, bunnies, but you can't hide!

STARLIGHT, STAR BRIGHT

The night sky is full of light. Especially on a cloudless night when it's sparkling with distant stars...

Orion

The Great Dog

Long ago, people thought the stars made pictures in the sky. They made up stories about them and gave them names.

North Star

Orion was a superhuman warrior in Greek mythology.

WOOF!

Up there is the NORTH STAR. It's bright enough to guide you NORTH in the darkness.

Ooohhhh!

The Moon

You might see JUPITER, a nearby planet. It's like Earth but much bigger and colder.

One of the lights you can see is the International Space Station.

This is the Milky Way galaxy. A galaxy is a group of millions of stars and planets.

ZOOOOM

A shooting star isn't a star at all. It's a ROCK burning up as it falls to Earth from space.

You might see the planet Venus, too.

I can see different things in the sky depending on where I am and what time of year it is.

This telescope is a HUGE eye for seeing faraway things. The Orion Nebula is so far away, even in our fastest space ship, it would take MILLIONS of years to get there.

OUTBACK

It's night in an Australian desert – the OUTBACK. It's very hot, so animals come out in the dark when it's cooler. Some of the ones here don't live ANYWHERE ELSE in the whole world.

NEOWWWWWWWWWW

I'm a doctor. The Outback is HUGE – flying is the quickest way to get to my patients.

So, who's out tonight?

AH-WOOO

AH-WOOO

A big pack of howling DINGOES! AH-WOOO!

Thousands of years ago, bilbies lived all over the Outback. But when people came to Australia, so did dingoes, foxes and cats. They hunted down bilbies and now there are only a few left.

Bilbies get all the water they need from eating BUGS.

Tasty treats for me.

Lonnnnng tongue

SLURP

Flowers close their petals to go to sleep at night. YAWN.

CITIES NEVER SLEEP

Big cities across the world are WIDE AWAKE, too. And after a day of work or study, people go out to enjoy themselves. Anything and everything is happening...

Some artists and writers work while the night goes on outside.

Ideas! I need more ideas!

It feels SPOOKY going to the museum at night!

Museums and art galleries open on some nights for people who are busy in the day.

In cities in HOT countries, people go out dancing at night when it's cooler.

I love to dance the salsa or the tango!

How was your day?

Mmmm, the food here is delicious.

Some cities have parades of fireworks and torches.

It's even dark enough for a LANTERN FESTIVAL.

AT NIGHT, cities are full of MUSIC.

Opera is VERY LONG, so it doesn't finish until LATE.

At karaoke, people try to entertain EACH OTHER by singing songs.

Jazz music STARTS late, for people who are NIGHT OWLS.

IS THERE NIGHT IN SPACE?

Not exactly, but it's always dark. It looks like night ALL THE TIME on the INTERNATIONAL SPACE STATION.

> Yawn! Well, my watch says it's 11 o'clock at night in my hometown.

> I'll turn down the temperature and the lights so we can all have a good sleep.

The station goes all the way around Earth once every 90 minutes. That means the astronauts see 16 sunsets and 16 sunrises EVERY 24 hours (an Earth day). They have to make their own bedtime.

> From the station, astronauts can see the WHOLE WORLD.

The SUN is coming up.

This is what the AURORA looks like from space.

This light is the line between night and day. It's called THE TERMINATOR.

The Earth is NEVER really dark. Look at all the lights!

The night is lit up by all the streetlights and buildings.

GOOD MORNING!

At the end of every night, the Sun comes up and the next day begins.

PEEP PEEP!

Wake up, birds!

Very busy and important cats arrive home.

Some people are already working.

First walkies of the day.

RRRROW WOW

It's bedtime for foxes and owls. YAWN.

Babies wake up early. VERY early.

Whirrrrr

BEEP BEEP!

ARRRRRRGH!

Whizzing along! WATCH ME GO! Fastest person aliiiiive! Doo-dee-doo!

INDEX

Aequorea jellyfish, 15
Arctic foxes, 20-21
Arctic hares, 20-21
astronauts, 28-29
Aurora, 20-21, 29
Australia, 24

bakeries, 5, 31
bearded pigs, 17
beetles, 19
bilbies, 24
birds, 4, 8-9, 21, 25, 30
buses, 5, 11, 31

chickens, 9
cities, 26-27
clouded leopards, 16
coral, 14-15
countryside, 8-9
cranes, 12-13

desert, 24-25
dingoes, 24
doctors, 4-5, 24, 31

emperor moths, 8

factories, 6-7
fireflies, 19
flowers, 17, 24
forests, 16-17, 18, 19
foxes, 4, 8-9, 20-21, 24, 30

Great Dog, the, 22
greater mouse deer, 17

hedgehogs, 8
Hose's civets, 17
hospitals, 5, 31

International Space Station, 23, 28

Julpan, 25
Jupiter, 23

koalas, 25

markets, 5, 31
mice, 4, 8, 25
Milky Way, the, 23
Moon, the, 3, 5, 22
moths, 8
museums, 26
music, 26-27

North Star, the, 22

octopuses, 15
Orion, 22, 25
Orion Nebula, 23
Outback, 24-25
owls, 4, 8, 20-21

pangolins, 17
phytoplankton, 18
planes, 11, 24
police, 4
ports, 7, 10, 12-13
post offices, 5, 31
privet hawk moths, 8
pufferfish, 15

Quantula striata, 19

rabbits, 9,
Rafflesia, 17
reefs, 14-15
reindeer, 20-21
robots, 6-7

sea, 10, 12-13, 14-15, 18
sharks, 19

ships, 10, 12-13
shooting stars, 23
skeletons, 14
snails, 19
snakes, 16-17
snowy owls, 20-21
Southeast Asia, 19
space, 22-23, 28-29
stars, 22-23, 25, 28-29
sugar gliders, 25
summer, 21
Sun, the, 2, 4-5, 21, 28, 31
sun bears, 17

tarsiers, 16
tawny frogmouths, 25
telescopes, 23
Terminator, the, 29
towns, 4-5, 30-31
trains, 10-11
trucks, 7, 10, 12-13

Venus, 23

waves, 14-15, 18
winter, 20
woods, 8, 19

INTERNET LINKS

Thank you to KUKA for permission to use images of their robots. KUKA is a leading global supplier of intelligent automation solutions. KUKA offer their customers in the automotive, electronics, consumer goods, metalworking, logistics/e-commerce, healthcare, education and service robotics industries everything they need from a single source: from components and cells to fully automated systems. The KUKA Group is headquartered in Augsburg.

Series editor: Ruth Brocklehurst
Managing designer: Nicola Butler
Digital manipulation: John Russell & Nick Wakeford

Expert advice from John and Margaret Rostron and Dr. Annabel Banks